CONTENTS GEORGE GERSHWIN'S GREATEST HITS

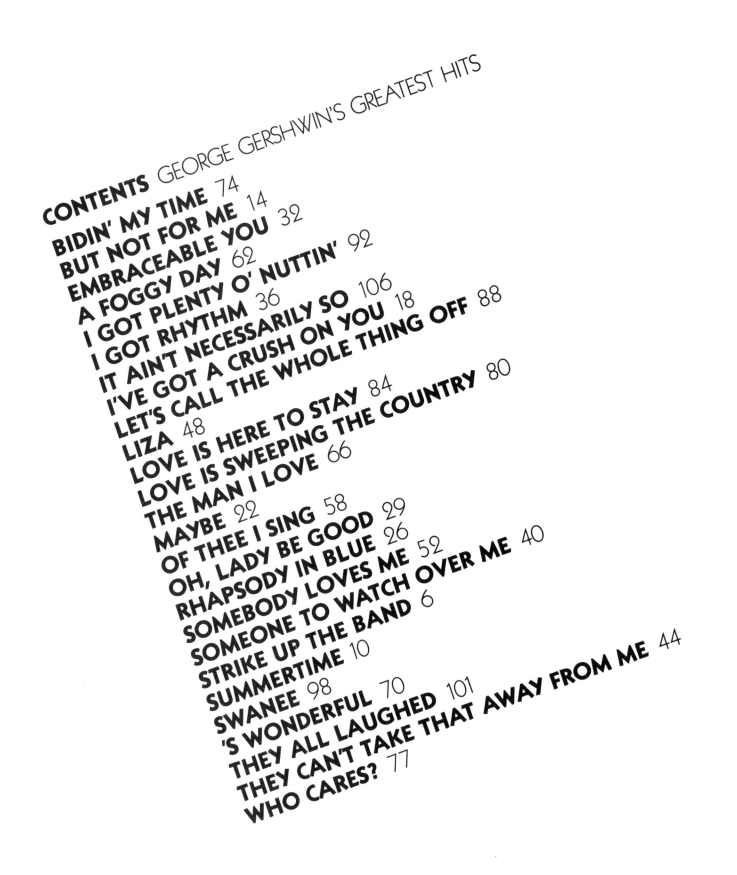

BIDIN' MY TIME 74
BUT NOT FOR ME 14
EMBRACEABLE YOU 32
A FOGGY DAY 62
I GOT PLENTY O' NUTTIN' 92
I GOT RHYTHM 36
IT AIN'T NECESSARILY SO 106
I'VE GOT A CRUSH ON YOU 18
LET'S CALL THE WHOLE THING OFF 88
LIZA 48
LOVE IS HERE TO STAY 84
LOVE IS SWEEPING THE COUNTRY 80
THE MAN I LOVE 66
MAYBE 22
OF THEE I SING 58
OH, LADY BE GOOD 29
RHAPSODY IN BLUE 26
SOMEBODY LOVES ME 52
SOMEONE TO WATCH OVER ME 40
STRIKE UP THE BAND 6
SUMMERTIME 10
SWANEE 98
'S WONDERFUL 70
THEY ALL LAUGHED 101
THEY CAN'T TAKE THAT AWAY FROM ME 44
WHO CARES? 77

IRA & GEORGE GERSHWIN

STRIKE UP THE BAND

Music and Lyrics by
GEORGE GERSHWIN
and IRA GERSHWIN

oth-er war But if we are forced in-to one The flag that we'll be

fight-ing for, Is the Red and White and Blue One! We do not fa-vor

war a-larms Rum-ta-ta-tum-tum-tum! But if we hear the

call to arms Rum-ta-ta-tum-tum, Rum-ta-ta-tum-tum, Rum-ta-ta-tum-tum-tum!

8

SUMMERTIME

(Lullaby)

By
GEORGE GERSHWIN,
DU BOSE and DOROTHY HEYWARD
and IRA GERSHWIN

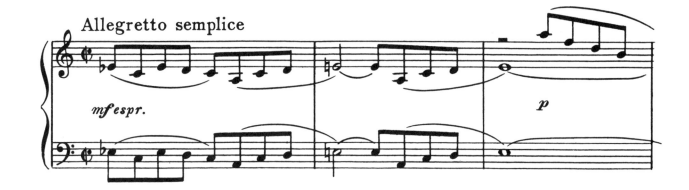

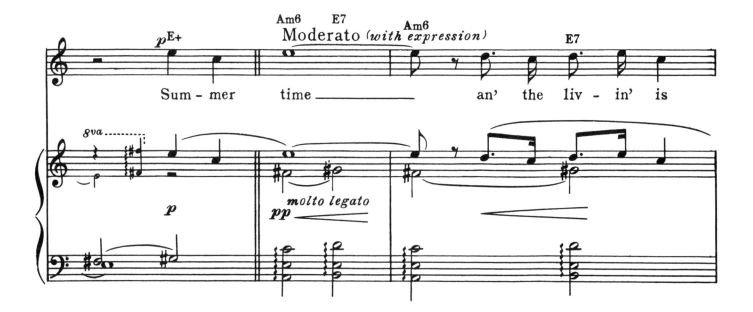

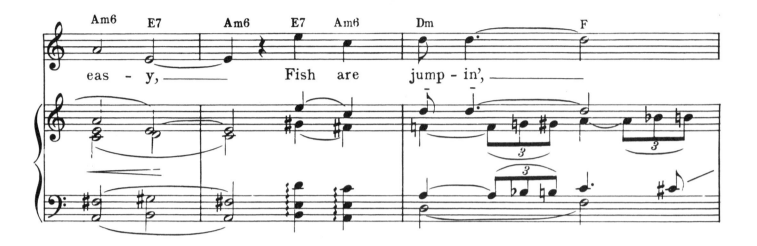

12

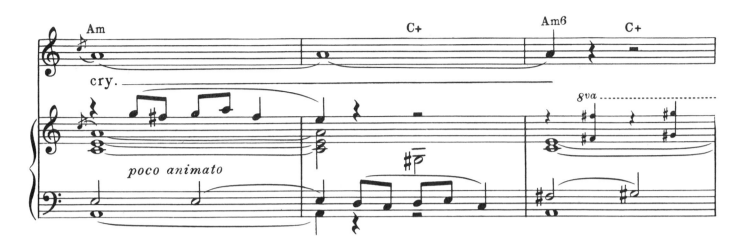

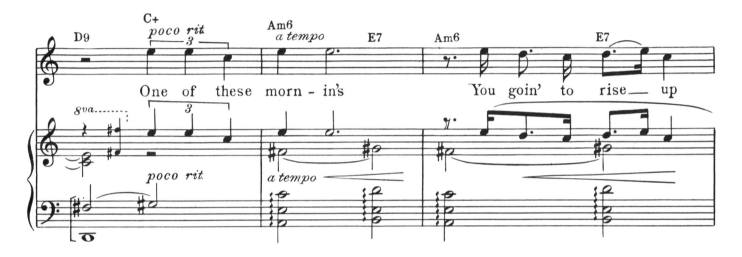

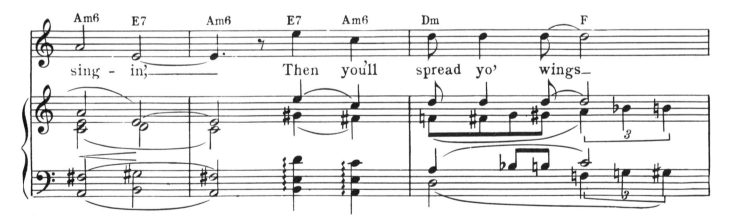

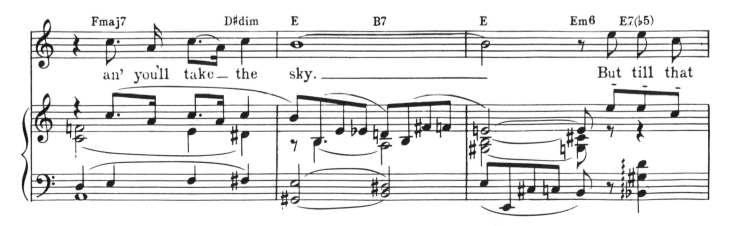

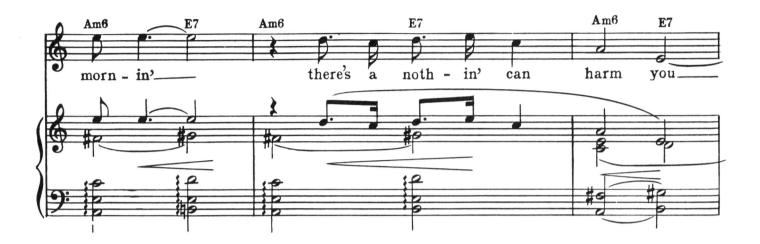

morn - in'_____ there's a noth - in' can harm you_____

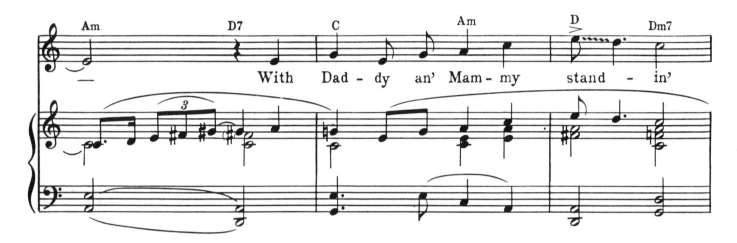

With Dad - dy an' Mam - my stand - in'

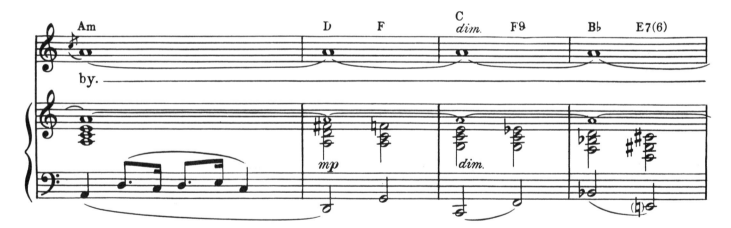

by._____

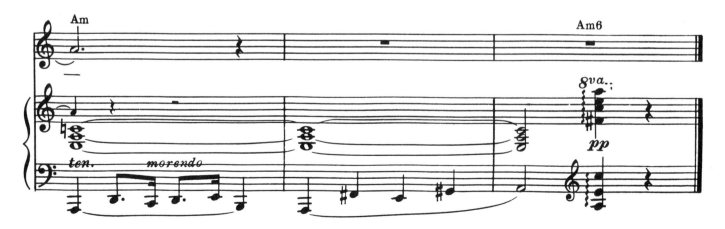

BUT NOT FOR ME

Music and Lyrics by
GEORGE GERSHWIN
and IRA GERSHWIN

Bea-trice Fair - fax, don't you dare Ev - er tell me he will care; I'm

cer - tain It's the fin - al cur-tain, I nev - er want to

hear From an - y cheer - ful Pol-ly - an - nas, Who tell you

fate, Sup-plies a mate; It's all ba - na - nas! They're writ - ing
(He's knock-ing)

16

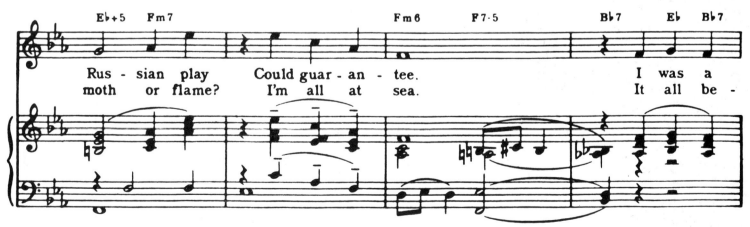

fool to fall___ And get that way; Heigh-ho! A - las! and al -
gan so well,___ But what an end! This is the time a fell -

- so, Lack - a - day! Al - though I can't dis - miss
- er needs a friend, When ev - 'ry hap - py plot

The mem - 'ry of his kiss, I guess he's not
Ends with the mar - riage knot, And there's no knot

for me. He's knock-ing
for me.___

I'VE GOT A CRUSH ON YOU

Music and Lyrics by
GEORGE GERSHWIN
and IRA GERSHWIN

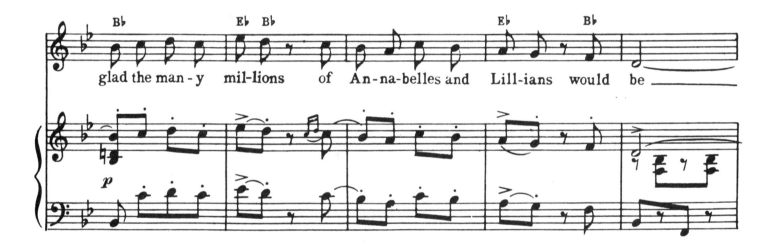

wore down my re - sist-ance: I fell,_____ and it was swell._____

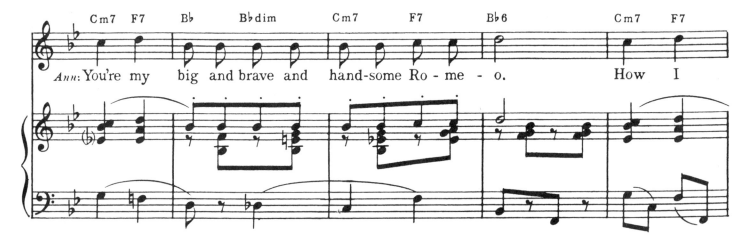

Ann: You're my big and brave and hand-some Ro - me - o. How I

won you I shall nev-er, nev-er know. *Timothy:* It's not that you're at - trac-tive, but,

oh my heart grew ac-tive, when you _____ came in - to view. _____

20

I've got 'a crush on you,___ sweet-ie pie,___

All the day and night-time hear me sigh.___ I

nev - er had ___ the least no - tion ___ that I could

fall with ___ so much e - mo - tion.___ Could you coo?

MAYBE

Music and Lyrics by
GEORGE GERSHWIN
and IRA GERSHWIN

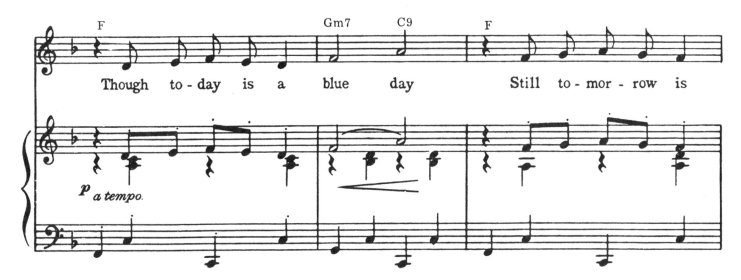

Though to-day is a blue day Still to-mor-row is

near, And per-haps with the new day

23

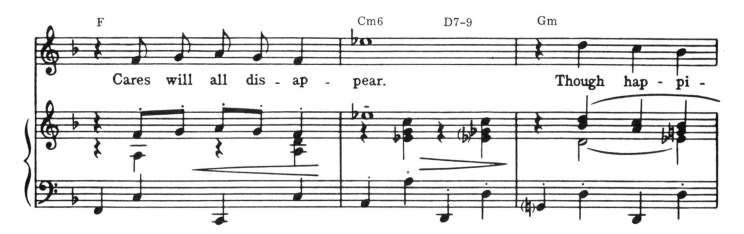

Cares will all dis - ap - pear. Though hap - pi -

ness is late, And we must wait, There's no need to be

ner - vous, There are dreams at your ser - vice.

Refrain

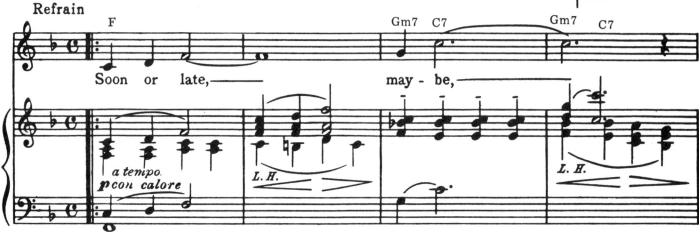

Soon or late,— may - be,—

24

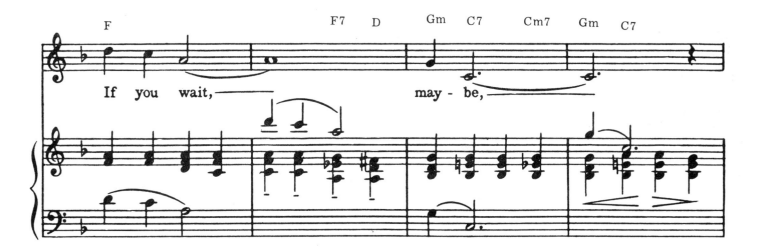

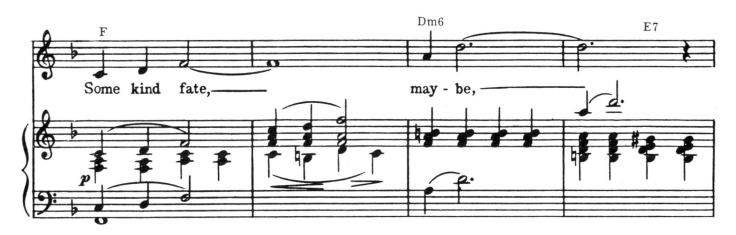

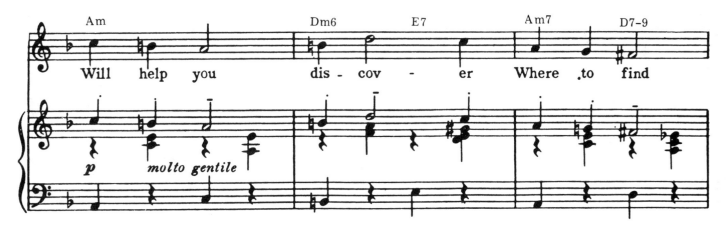

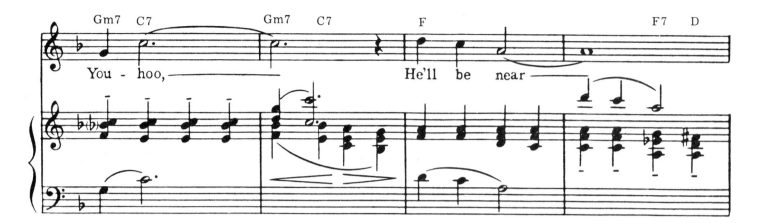

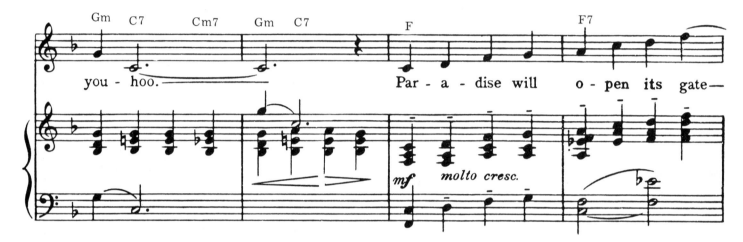

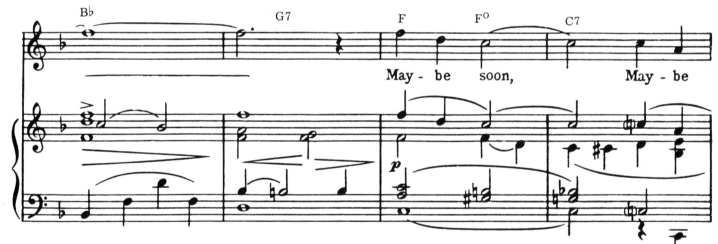

RHAPSODY IN BLUE

Music by
GEORGE GERSHWIN

Moderately slow, with expression

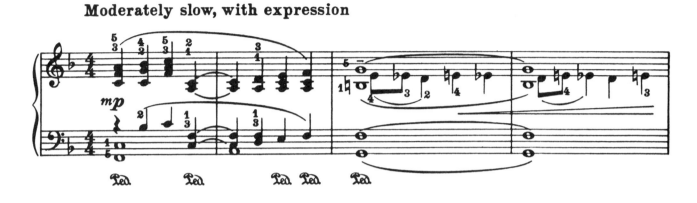

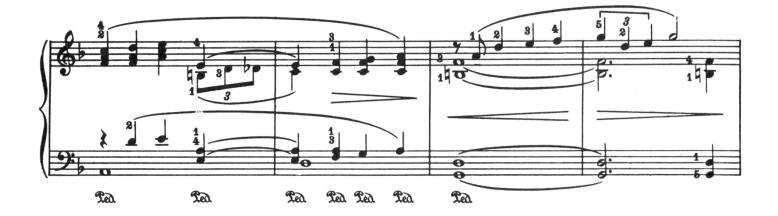

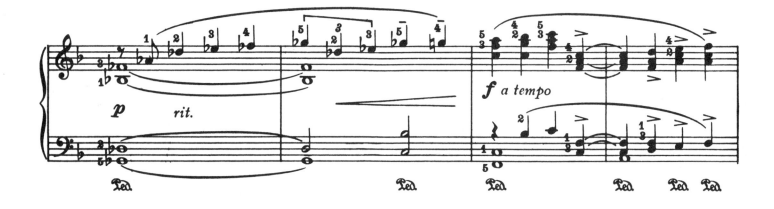

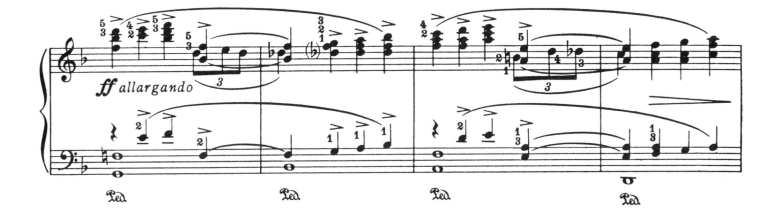

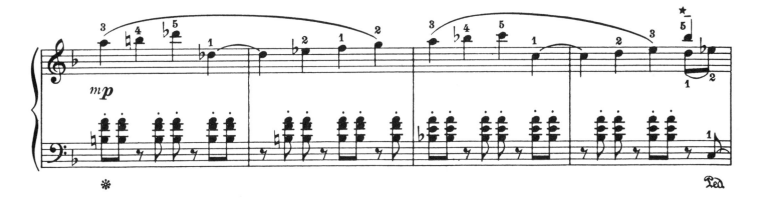

*Ending by arranger

OH, LADY BE GOOD!

Music and Lyrics by
GEORGE GERSHWIN
and IRA GERSHWIN

EMBRACEABLE YOU

Spanish Version by
JOHNNIE CAMACHO
French Version by
EMELIA RENAUD

Music and Lyrics by
GEORGE GERSHWIN
and IRA GERSHWIN

What was it that con-trolled___ me? What kept my love-life
Qu'est - ce qui m'a con-tro - - lé? Et gar - dé mon a -
Quie - ro que tú meex-pli - ques, Qué_es lo que de - bo ha -

lean? My in - tu - i - tion told___ me You'd come
mour? Si ce n'est que la pen - - sée De te
cer? Cuan - do yo quie - ro ver - - te, No me

on the scene. La - dy, lis - ten to the rhy - thm of my
voir un jour. De mon cœur é - cou - tes les bat - te - ments
quie - res ver, Cuan - do no te_a - bra - zo, quie - res que te_a -

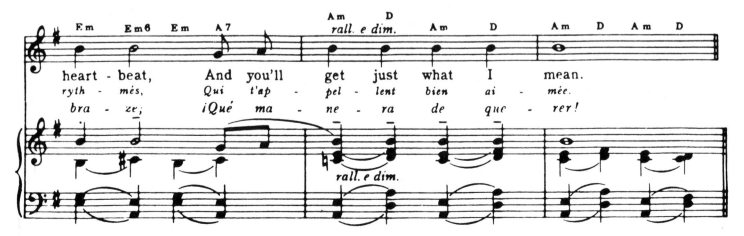

heart - beat, And you'll get just what I mean.
ryth - més, Qui t'ap - pel - lent bien ai - mée.
bra - ze; ¡Qué ma - ne - ra de que - rer!

REFRAIN *Rhythmically*

Em-brace me,
My sweet em - brace - a - ble you!____
*Un bai - ser,
mon a - do - ra - ble pou-pée!____
Tea - bra - zo
con to - da mi de - vo - ción.____*

Em-brace me,
You ir - re - place - a - ble you!____
*Un bai - ser,
Ir - ré - sis - ti - ble beau - té!____
Tea - bra - zo
y,en - tre - go mi co - ra - zón.____*

Just one look at you, my heart grew tip - sy in me;____
*Un re - gard de toi peut faire cha - vi - rer mon coeur,____
Te - mo tan - to que no me co - rres - pon - de - rás,____*

You and you a - lone bring out the gyp - sy in me!____
*Je sais que toi seu - le peut fai - re mon bon - heur!____
Que mis an - sias nun - ca, nun - ca com - pren - de - rás.____*

I love all the man-y charms a-bout you;
J'ai - me tout ce qui me par - le de toi;
Me a - bra - zas sin de - mos - trar e - mo - ción.

A - bove all I want my arms a-bout you. Don't be a
En - core plus je te veux tout pres de moi. Ne sois pas
Me be - sas con tan es - ca - sa i - lu - sión. No sé si

naugh-ty ba - by, Come to pa-pa, Come to pa-pa, do! My sweet em-
si mé - chan - te, Viens mon chou-chou, viens mon chou-chou, viens! Mon a - do -
de boa - mar - te, Pe - ro pa - ra de - mos - trar mi a - mor, Te a - bra - za -

brace - a - ble you! you!
ra - ble pou - pée! pée!
ré por los dos. dos.

I GOT RHYTHM

Music and Lyrics by
GEORGE GERSHWIN
and IRA GERSHWIN

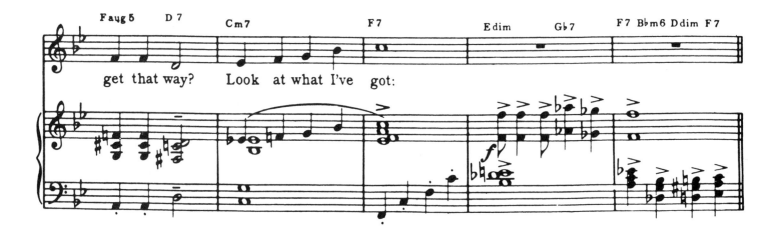

REFRAIN (*with abandon*)

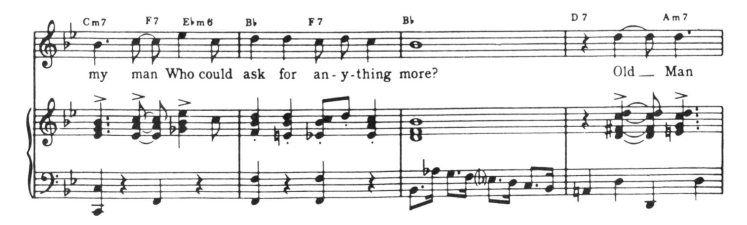

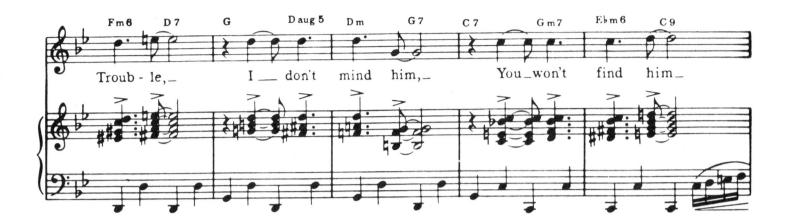

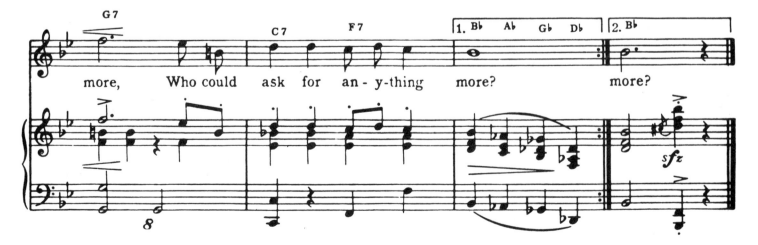

SOMEONE TO WATCH OVER ME

French Version by
EMELIA RENAUD

Music and Lyrics by
GEORGE GERSHWIN
and IRA GERSHWIN

There's a say-ing old Says that love is blind, Still we're of-ten told, "Seek and
Un pro-ver-be dit l'a-mour a - veu-glé, *On nous dit aus-si: "Cher-chez*

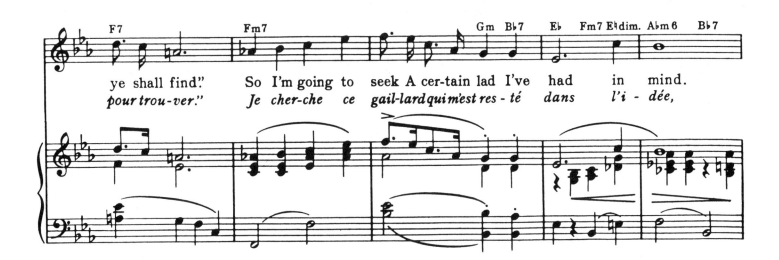

ye shall find." So I'm going to seek A cer-tain lad I've had in mind.
pour trou-ver." *Je cher-che ce gail-lard qui m'est res - té dans l'i - dée,*

Look-ing ev-'ry-where, Have-n't found him yet; He's the big af-fair I can-
Re - gar-dant par-tout sans le ren - con-trer; C'est un gars que je ne puis

not for-get. On - ly man I ev - er Think of with re - gret.
ou - bli - er. Le seul homme à qui je pense a - vec re - gret.

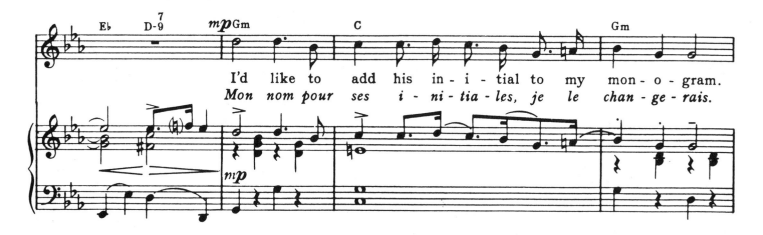

I'd like to add his in-i-tial to my mon-o-gram.
Mon nom pour ses i - ni-tia-les, je le chan-ge-rais.

Tell me, where is the shep-herd for this lost lamb.
Pour la bre - bis per-due, où est le ber - ger?

un poco rall.

42

REFRAIN

There's a some-bod-y I'm long-ing to see. I hope that he Turns out to be
Il est un quel-qu'un que je veux re-voir Cha-que ma-tin et cha - que soir,

Some-one who'll watch o - ver me._____ I'm a lit - tle lamb who's
Et qui me pro - té-ge - ra._____ Je suis la bre-bis per-

lost in the wood. I know I could Al-ways be good To one who'll
due dans le bois. Je don - ne-rai Tou-te ma foi A qui me

watch o - ver me._____ Al-though he may not be the
pro - té-ge - ra._____ Quoi-qu'il ne soit pas un hom -

THEY CAN'T TAKE THAT AWAY FROM ME

Music and Lyrics by
GEORGE GERSHWIN
and IRA GERSHWIN

The way your smile just beams,___ The way you sing off key,___

The way you haunt my dreams,___ No, no! They can't take that a-way from me!___

We may nev-er, nev-er meet a-gain On the bump-y road to

love, Still I'll al-ways, al-ways keep the mem-'ry of

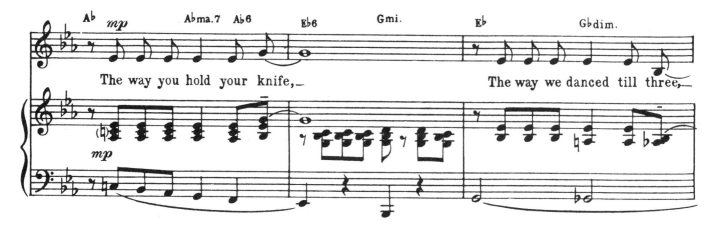

LIZA (All The Clouds'll Roll Away)

Words by
IRA GERSHWIN and GUS KAHN

Music by
GEORGE GERSHWIN

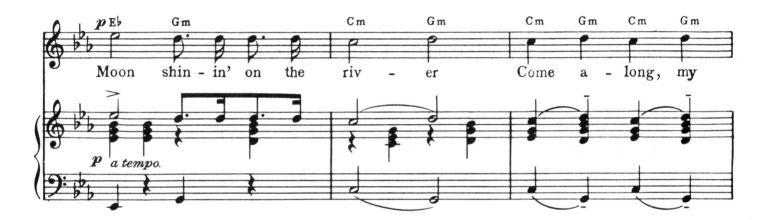

Moon shin-in' on the riv - er Come a - long, my

Li - za! Breeze sing-in' through the tree - tops

Come a - long, my Li - za! Some-thin' might-y sweet I want to

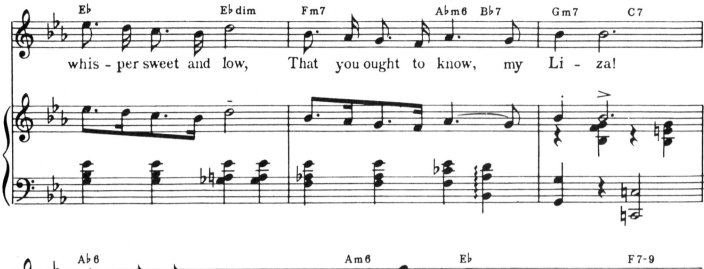

whis - per sweet and low, That you ought to know, my Li - za!

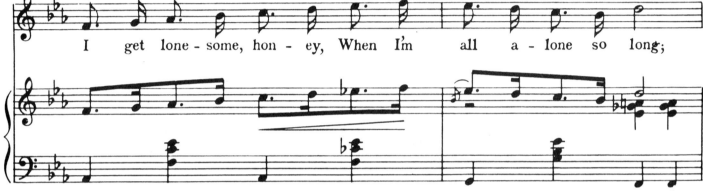

I get lone - some, hon - ey, When I'm all a - lone so long;

Don't make me wait; Don't hes - i - tate; Come and hear my song:

Refrain

Li - za, Li - za, skies are gray,

But if you'll smile on me All the clouds-'ll roll a-

way. Li - za, Li - za, don't de -

lay, Come, keep me com-pa-ny, And the clouds-'ll roll a-

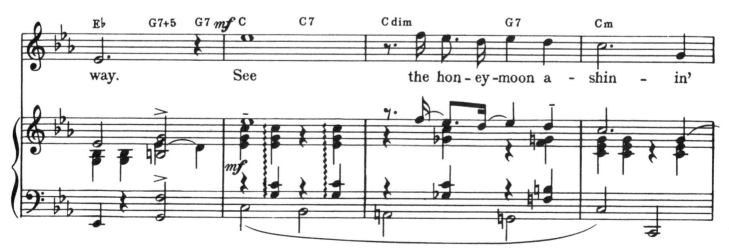

way. See the hon-ey-moon a - shin - in'

down; We should make a date with

Par - son Brown. So, Li - za, Li - za,

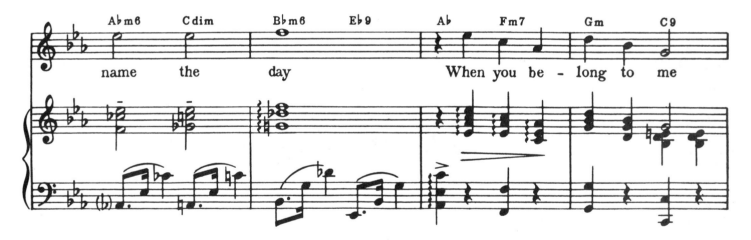

name the day When you be - long to me

And the clouds-'ll roll a - way. - way.

SOMEBODY LOVES ME

Words by
BALLARD MACDONALD and B. G. DE SYLVA
French version by EMELIA RENAUD

Music by
GEORGE GERSHWIN

54

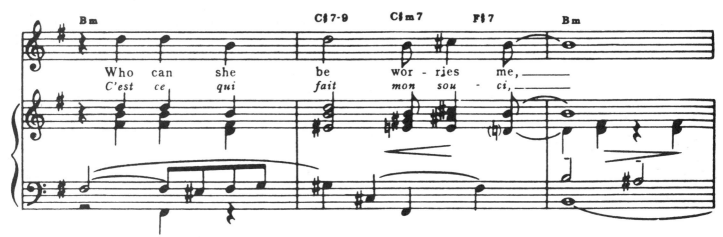

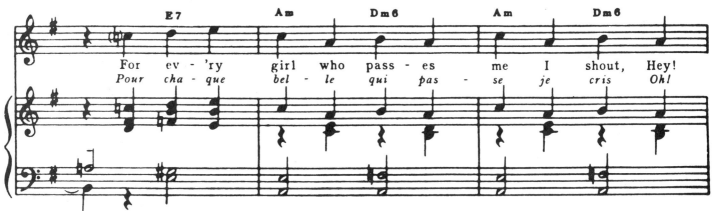

may - be,
la!
be,
la!
You were meant to be my lov - ing
Se - rait el - le par ha - zard mon

ba - by;
a - mie?
Some - bod - y loves me
Quel - qu'un m'ai - me - ra

I won - der who,
Je ne sais qui;
May - be it's
Peut - ê - tre

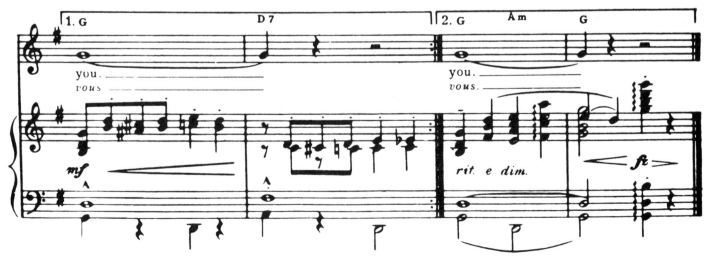

you.
vous.
you.
vous.

IRA GERSHWIN

GEORGE GERSHWIN

OF THEE I SING

Music and Lyrics by
GEORGE GERSHWIN
and IRA GERSHWIN

Assai moderato

From the Is - land of Man - hat - tan to the Coast of Gold, From North to

South, From East to West, You are the love I love the best.

59

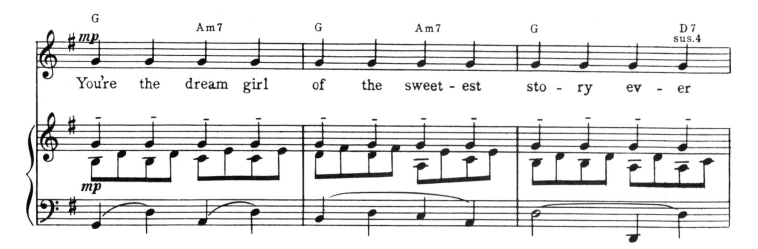

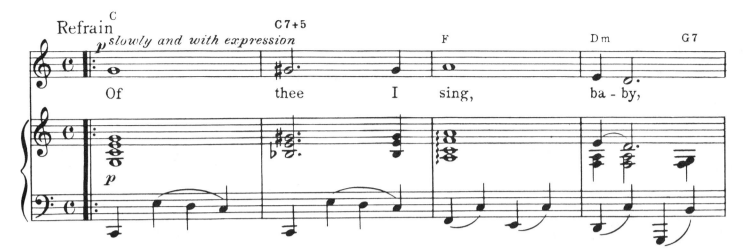

Refrain *slowly and with expression*

Of thee I sing, ba - by,

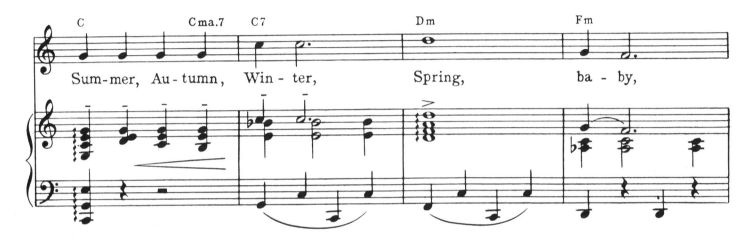

Sum - mer, Au - tumn, Win - ter, Spring, ba - by,

You're my sil - ver lin - ing, You're my sky of blue;

There's a love light shin - ing, Just be - cause of you.

A FOGGY DAY

Music and Lyrics by
GEORGE GERSHWIN
and IRA GERSHWIN

I was a strang-er in the cit-y.___ Out of town were the peo-ple I knew.

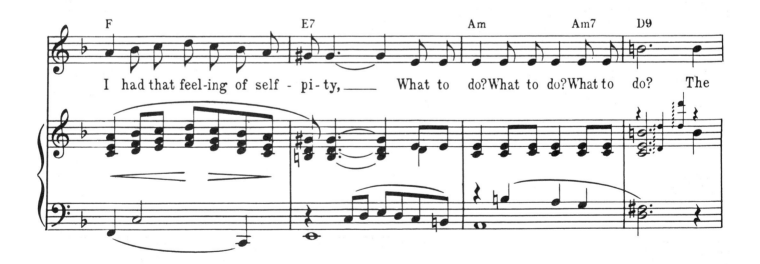

I had that feel-ing of self - pi-ty,___ What to do? What to do? What to do? The

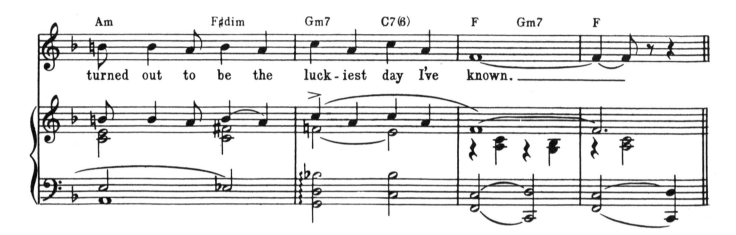

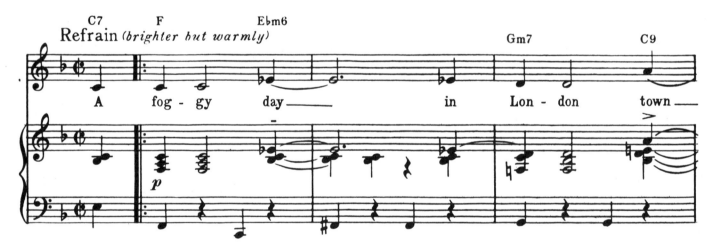

64

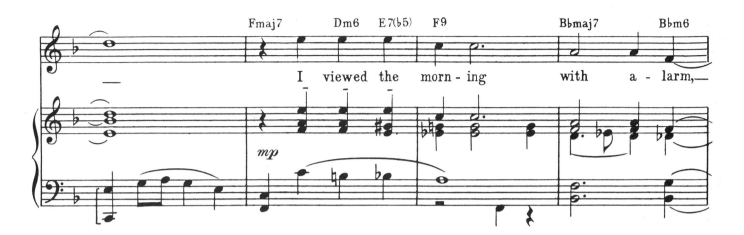

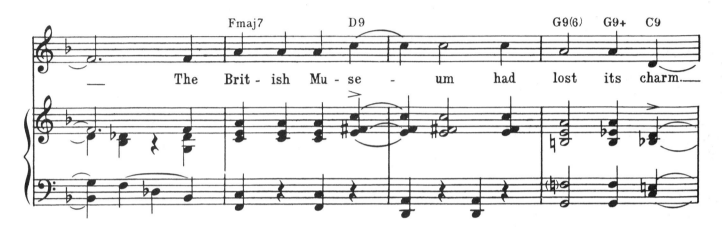

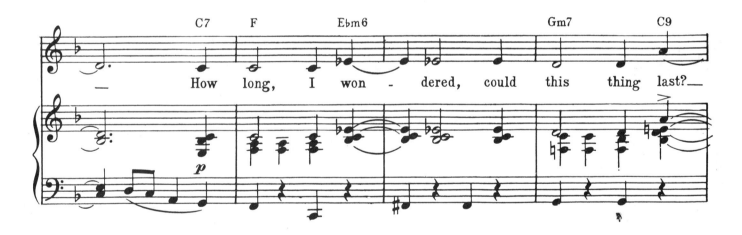

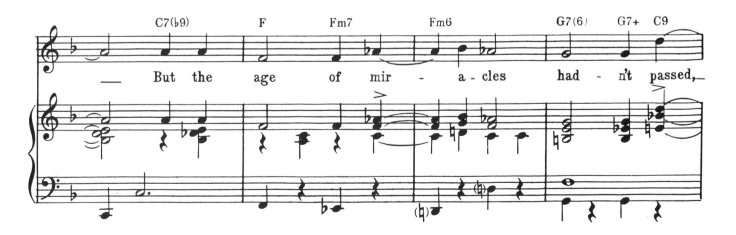

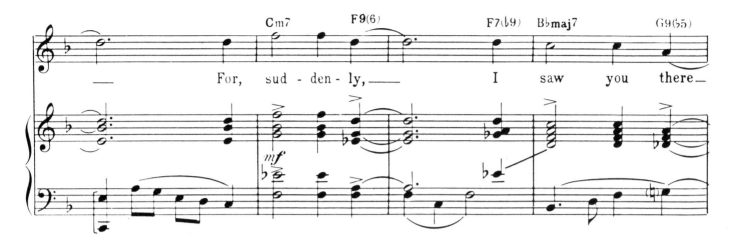

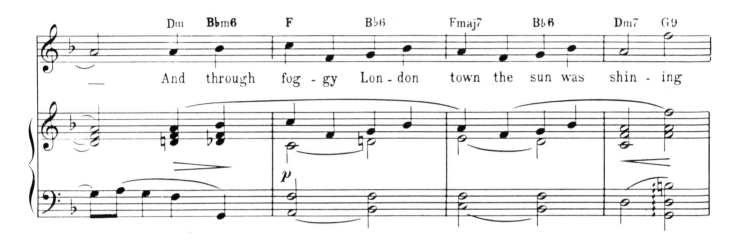

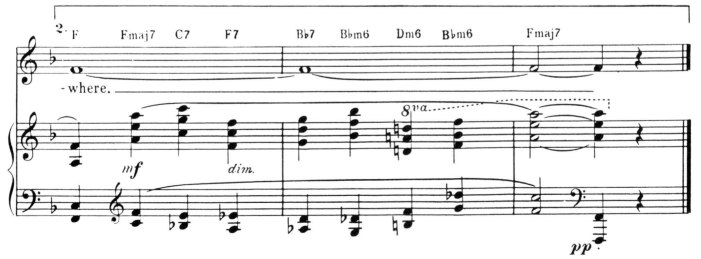

THE MAN I LOVE

French Version by
EMELIA RENAUD
Spanish Version by
JOHNNIE CAMACHO

Music and Lyrics by
GEORGE GERSHWIN
and IRA GERSHWIN

When the mel-low moon be-gins to beam, Ev-'ry night I
Fr. Quand la lu-ne mon-te dou-ce-ment, Cha-que soir je
Sp. Mien-tras bri-llen en el cie-lo a-zul Las es-tre-llas

dream a lit-tle dream, And of course Prince Charm-ing is the theme The
rê-ve d'oi-seaux bleus; D'un Prin-ce Char-mant tout ray-on-nant Com-
y la lu-na gris, Pa-sa-ré las no-ches, sin dor-mir, Por

he for me. Al-though I re-al-ize as well as you,
blant mes voeux. Quoi-que je sache tout aus-si bien que vous
la se-ñal. Pués sé que un di-a tie-ne que ve-nir,

'S WONDERFUL

Music and Lyrics by
GEORGE GERSHWIN
and IRA GERSHWIN

Life has just be - gun.
Don't mind tell - ing you,

Jack has found his Jill,
In my hum - ble fash,

Don't know what you've done,
That you thrill me through

But I'm all a - thrill.
With a ten - der pash.

How can words ex - press   Your di - vine ap - peal?
When you said you care,   'Mag - ine my e - mosh;

You can nev - er   guess   All the love I   feel.
I swore then and   there   Per - ma - nent de - vosh.

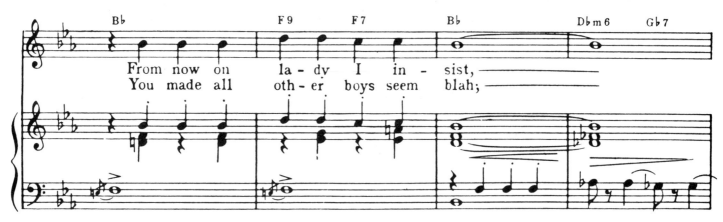

From now on   la - dy I in - sist,
You made all   oth - er boys seem   blah;

For me no   oth - er girls ex - ist.
Just you a   lone filled me with   Aah!

un poco rit.

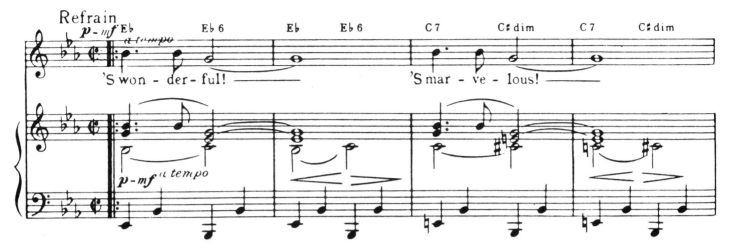

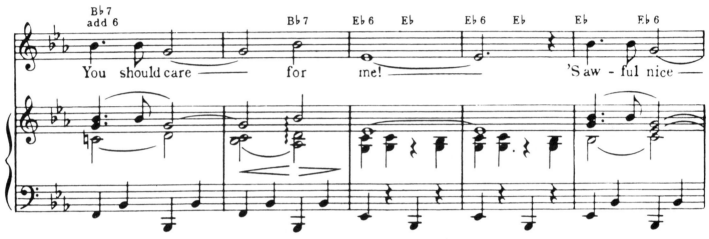

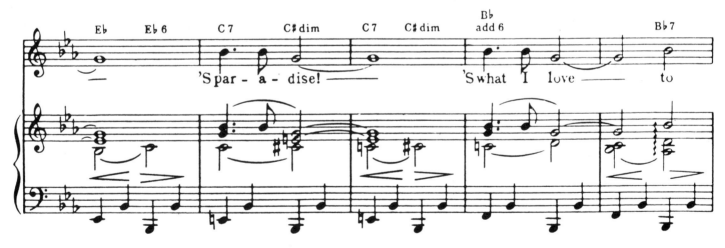

73

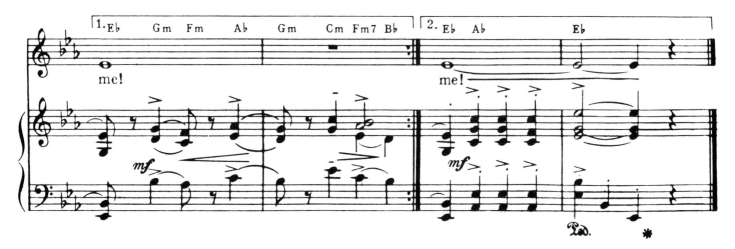

BIDIN' MY TIME

Music and Lyrics by
GEORGE GERSHWIN
and IRA GERSHWIN

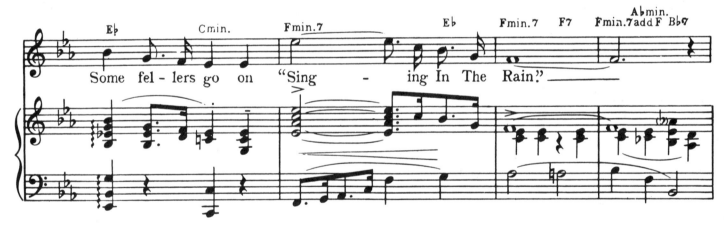

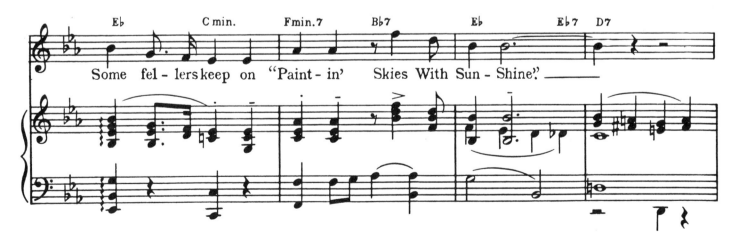

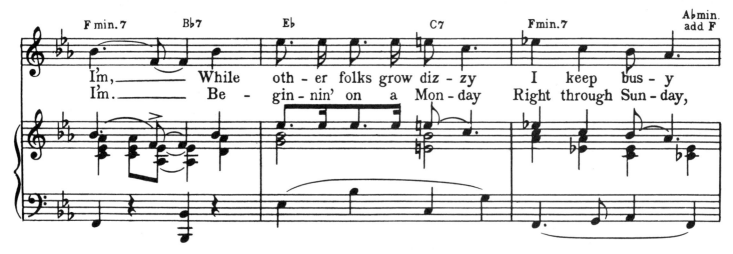

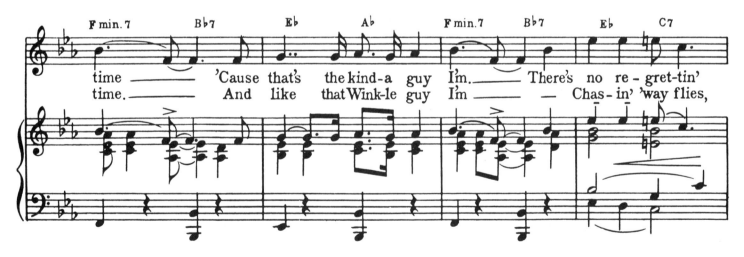

WHO CARES?

Music and Lyrics by
GEORGE GERSHWIN
and IRA GERSHWIN

I love you and you love me And that's how it will al-ways be, And noth-ing else can

ev - er mean a thing._____ Who cares what the pub - lic

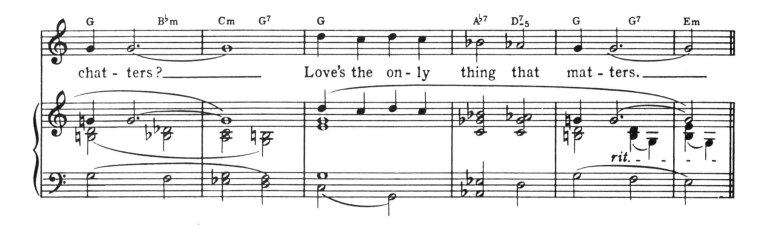

chat - ters?_____ Love's the on - ly thing that mat - ters._____

REFRAIN, *(in a lilting manner)*

WHO CARES If the sky cares to fall in the sea?_____

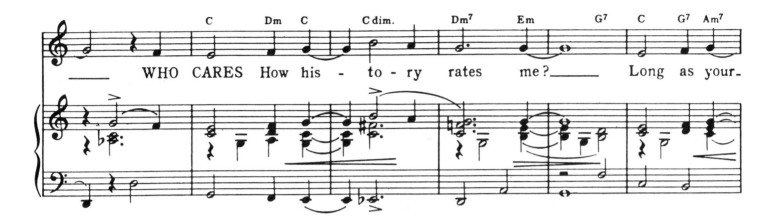

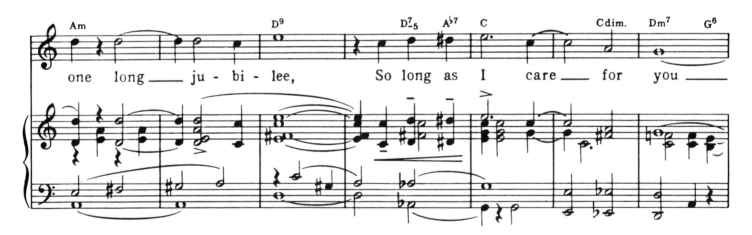

LOVE IS SWEEPING THE COUNTRY

Music and Lyrics by
GEORGE GERSHWIN
and IRA GERSHWIN

Why are peo - ple gay All the night and day, Feel-ing as they

nev - er felt be - fore? What is the thing That makes them sing?

Rich man, poor man, thief, Doc - tor, law - yer, chief,

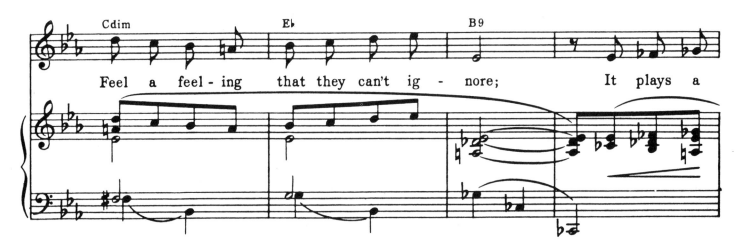

Feel a feel - ing that they can't ig - nore; It plays a

part In ev - 'ry heart, And ev - 'ry

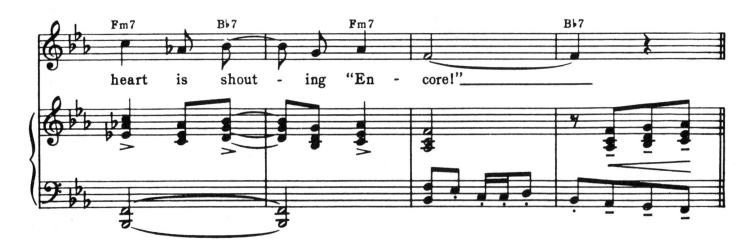

heart is shout - ing "En - core!"

REFRAIN

LOVE IS SWEEP-ING THE COUN-TRY, _____ Waves are hug-

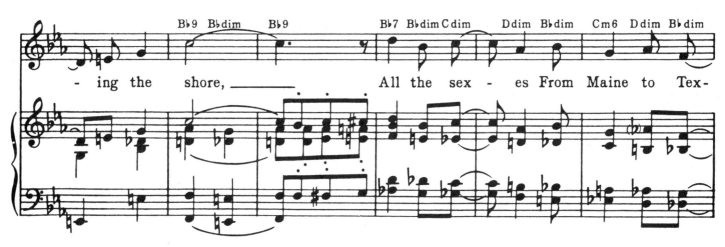

-ing the shore, _____ All the sex - es From Maine to Tex-

- as Have nev - er known such love be - fore. _____

See them bill - ing and coo-ing, _____ Like the bird-

LOVE IS HERE TO STAY

Words by
IRA GERSHWIN

Music by
GEORGE GERSHWIN

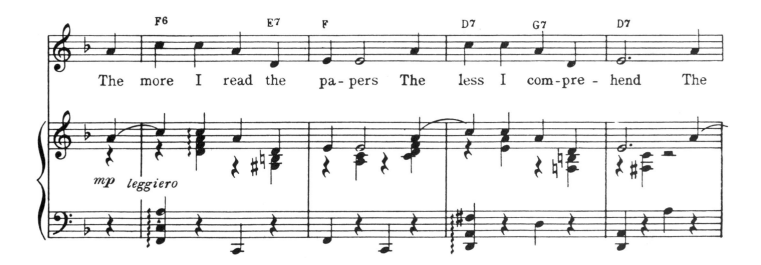

The more I read the pa-pers The less I com-pre-hend The

world and all its ca-pers And how it all will end. Noth-ing seems to be

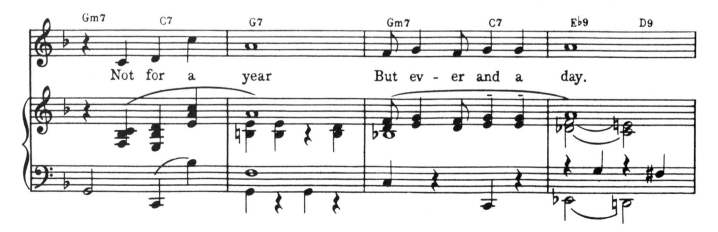

The ra - di - o and the tel - e - phone and the

mov - ies that we know May just be pass - ing fan - cies,

And in time may go. But, oh my dear,

Our love is here to stay; To - geth - er

we're go - ing a long, long way.

In time the Rock - ies may crum - ble, Gib - ral - tar may tum - ble,

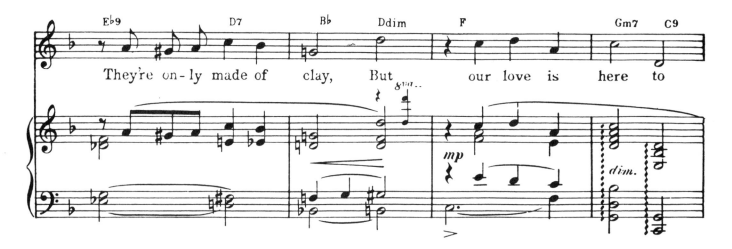

They're on - ly made of clay, But our love is here to

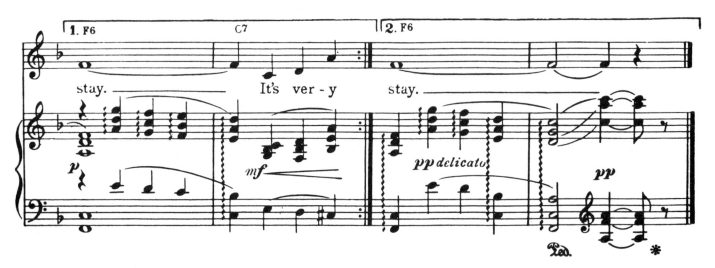

stay. It's ver - y stay.

LET'S CALL THE WHOLE THING OFF

Music and Lyrics by
GEORGE GERSHWIN
and IRA GERSHWIN

Things have come to a pret-ty pass, Our ro-mance is grow-ing flat, For

you like this and the oth-er While I go for this and that.

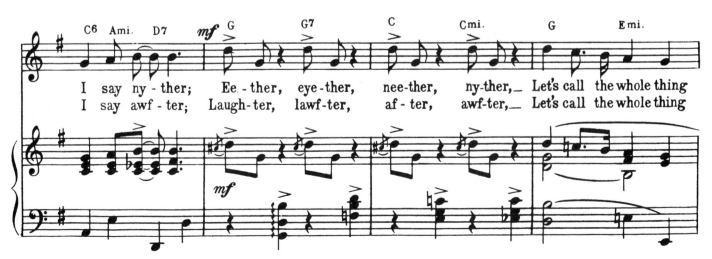

off!   You like po-ta-to and I like po-tah-to,   You like to-ma-to and
off!   You like va-nil-la and I like va-nel-la,   You, sa's'-pa-ril-la and

I like to-mah-to; Po-ta-to, Po-tah-to, To-ma-to, To-mah-to!
I sa's'-pa-rel-la; Va-nil-la, va-nel-la, __ Choc'-late, __ straw-b'ry!

Let's call the whole thing off!   But   oh!   If we call the whole thing

off, Then we must part.   And oh!   If we ev-er part, Then

that might break my heart! So, if you like pa-ja-mas And I like pa-jah-mas,
So, if you go for oyst-ers And I go for erst-ers

I'll wear pa-ja-mas and give up pa-jah-mas.
I'll or-der oyst-ers and can-cel the erst-ers. For we know we

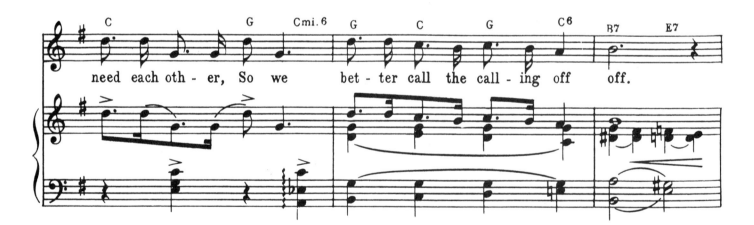

need each oth-er, So we bet-ter call the call-ing off off.

Let's call the whole thing off! _____ off! _____

I GOT PLENTY O' NUTTIN'

By
GEORGE GERSHWIN,
DU BOSE and DOROTHY HEYWARD
and IRA GERSHWIN

Allegretto

Moderato

Porgy: Oh I got plen-ty o' nut-tin', ___ An' nut-tin's plen - ty fo'

me. I got no car, got no mule, I got no mis-er - y. ___

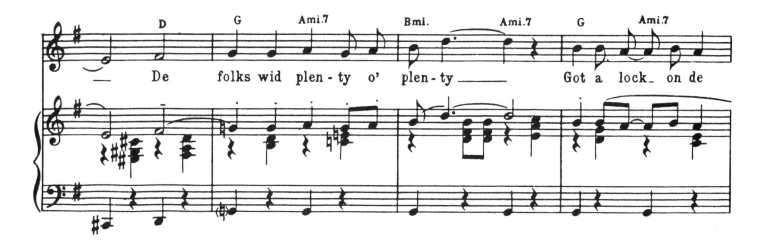

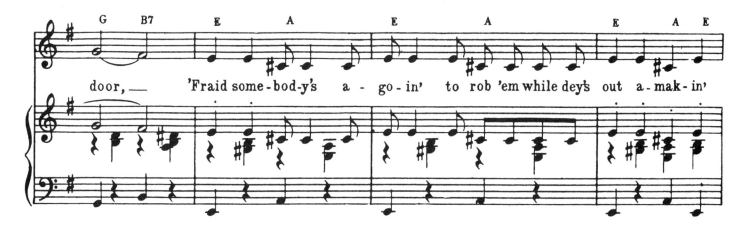

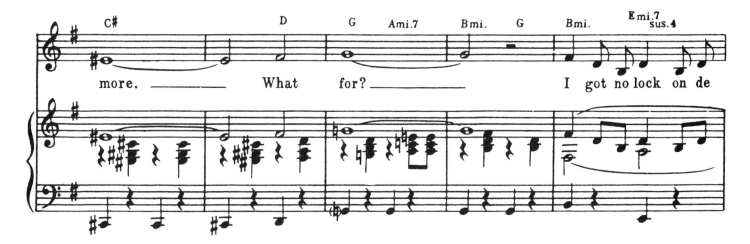

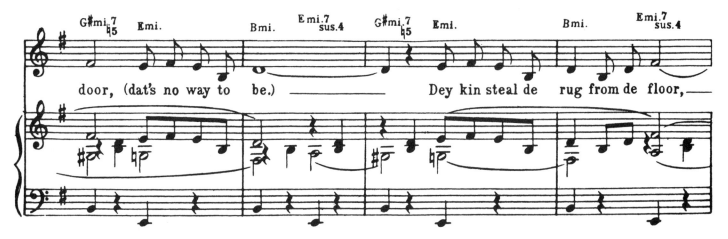

Dat's o-keh wid me, 'Cause de things dat I prize, Like de stars in de skies, all are free.

Oh, I got plen-ty o' nut-tin', An' nut-tin's plen-ty fo' me. I

got my gal, got my song, got Heb-ben the whole day long.

(Spoken in high voice)
No use com-plain-in'! Got my gal, got my Lawd,

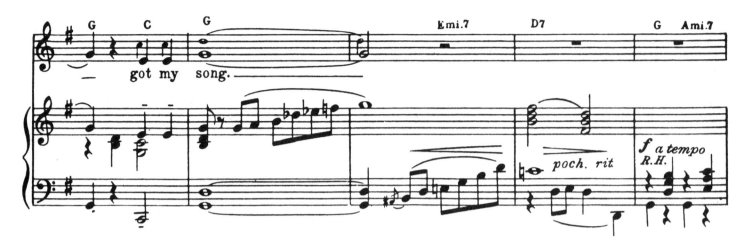

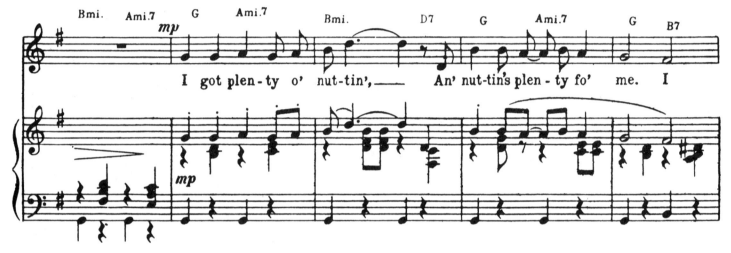

Seems wid plen-ty you sure got to wor-ry how to keep the deb-ble a-way, _____

— a - way. _____ I ain't a-fret-tin' 'bout hell Till de time ar-

rive. _____ Nev-er wor-ry long as I'm well, _____ Nev-er one to

strive to be good, to be bad, What the hell? I is glad I's a-live. _____ Oh,

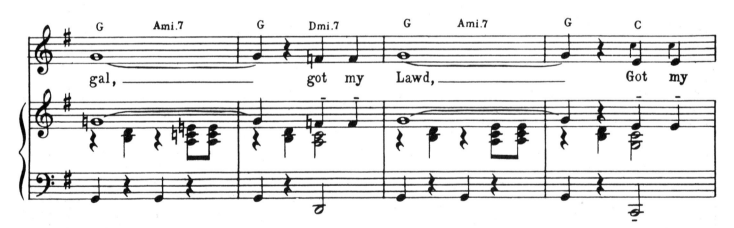

SWANEE

Words by
IRVING CAESAR

Music by
GEORGE GERSHWIN

THEY ALL LAUGHED

Music and Lyrics by
GEORGE GERSHWIN
and IRA GERSHWIN

peo - ple from Mis - sou - ri nev - er in - censed me. ___

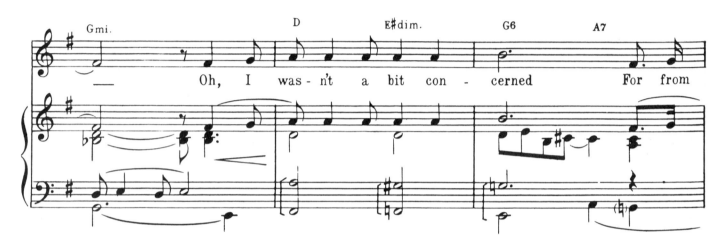

___ Oh, I was - n't a bit con - cerned For from

hist' - ry I had learned How man - y, man - y times the

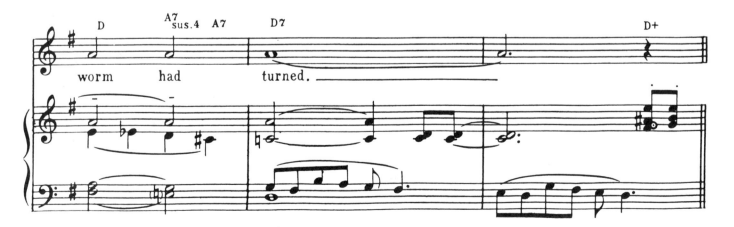

worm had turned. ___

They all laughed at Chris-to-pher Co-lum-bus When he said the World was round.
They all laughed at Rock- e -fel - ler Cen-ter Now they're fight - ing to get in.

They all laughed when Ed - i - son re - cord - ed sound.
They all laughed at Whit - ney and his cot - ton gin.

They all laughed at
They all laughed at

Wil - bur and his broth - er, When they said that man could fly.
Ful - ton and his steam - boat, Her - shey and his choc'- late bar.

104

They told Mar-co-ni Wire-less was a pho-ney;
Ford and his Liz-zie Kept the laugh-ers bus-y;

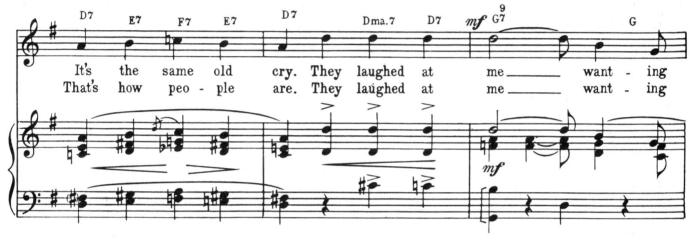

It's the same old cry. They laughed at me____ want-ing
That's how peo-ple are. They laughed at me____ want-ing

you,____ Said I was reach-ing for the moon; But
you,____ Said it would be Hel-lo, Good-bye; But

oh,____ You came through_ Now they'll have to change their tune.
oh,____ You came through_ Now they're eat-ing hum-ble pie.

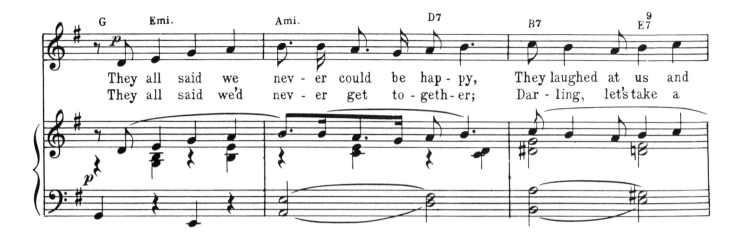

They all said we nev-er could be hap-py, They laughed at us and
They all said we'd nev-er get to-geth-er; Dar-ling, let's take a

how! But Ho, Ho, Ho! Who's got the last laugh
bow, For, Ho, Ho, Ho! Who's got the last laugh,

now?_____ He, He, He! Let's at the past laugh,

Ha, Ha, Ha! Who's got the last laugh now?_____

IT AIN'T NECESSARILY SO

By
GEORGE GERSHWIN,
DU BOSE and DOROTHY HEYWARD
and IRA GERSHWIN

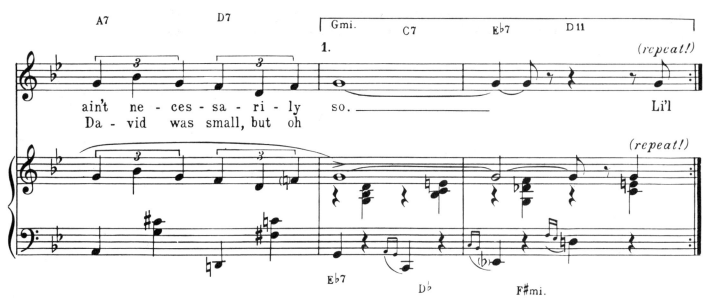

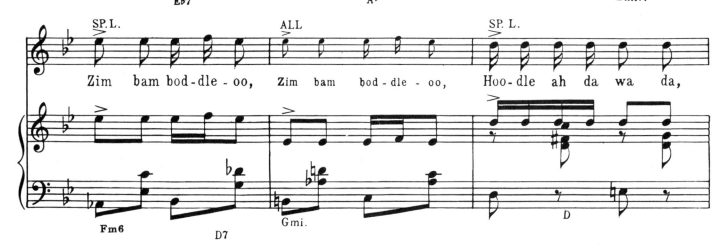

so._____ To get in - to Heb - ben don' snap for a seb - ben! Live

clean! Don' have no fault. Oh, I takes dat gos - pel When - ev - er it's pos' - ble, But

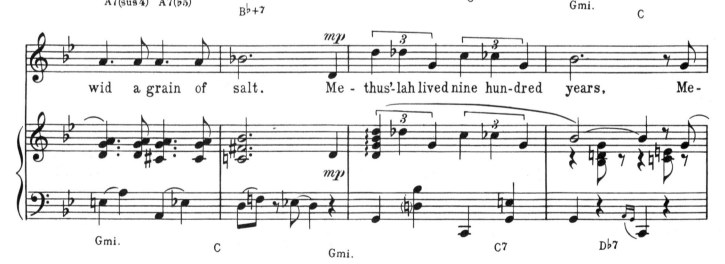

wid a grain of salt. Me - thus' - lah lived nine hun - dred years, Me -

thus - lah lived nine hun - dred years, But who calls dat liv - in' When

Major Works of GEORGE GERSHWIN Arranged for P★I★A★N★O

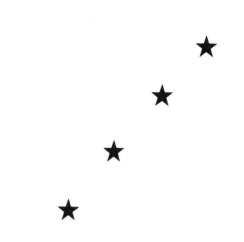

RHAPSODY IN BLUE

Piano Solo (based on original) (PS0047)
Piano Solo—Modified Version by Herman Wasserman (PS0048)
Piano Duet—Transcribed by Henry Levine (PS0157)
†Two Pianos-Four Hands (original setting) (PS0165)

AN AMERICAN IN PARIS

Piano Solo in Miniature—Transcribed by Maurice C. Whitne (PS0004)
Piano Solo—Transcribed by William Daly (PS0003)

CONCERTO IN F

Piano Solo—Transcribed by Grace Castagnetta (PS0017)
†Two Pianos-Four Hands (PS0161)

PRELUDES

Piano Solo (original setting) (PS0043)
Piano Duet—Transcribed by Gregory Stone (PS0156)
Two Pianos-Four Hands—Transcribed by Gregory Stone (PS0164)

CUBAN OVERTURE

Two Pianos-Four Hands—Transcribed by Gregory Stone (PS0162)

SECOND RHAPSODY

†Two Pianos-Four Hands (original setting) (PS0166)

†For Piano and Orchestra Orchestral part in reduction for second piano. Two copies necessary for performance.

Available at your local music dealer.

GEORGE GERSHWIN

GREATEST HITS